Conference of the North American Chapter of the Association for Computational Linguistics: Human Language Technologies (NAACL HLT 2019)

Tutorial Abstracts

Minneapolis, Minnesota, USA
2 – 7 June 2019

ISBN: 978-1-5108-8758-9

Printed from e-media with permission by:

Curran Associates, Inc.
57 Morehouse Lane
Red Hook, NY 12571

Printed by Curran Associates, Inc. (2019)

Association for Computational Linguistics
209 N. Eighth Street
Stroudsburg, Pennsylvania 18360

Phone: 1-570-476-8006
Fax: 1-570-476-0860

acl@aclweb.org

Additional copies of this publication are available from:

Curran Associates, Inc.
57 Morehouse Lane
Red Hook, NY 12571 USA
Phone: 845-758-0400
Fax: 845-758-2633
Email: curran@proceedings.com
Web: www.proceedings.com

NAACL HTL 2019

The 2019 Conference of the North American Chapter of the Association for Computational Linguistics: Human Language Technologies

Tutorial Abstracts

June 2 2019
Minneapolis, Minnesota

Introduction

Welcome to the Tutorials Session of NAACL HLT 2019 in Minneapolis, MN, USA.

The NAACL-HLT tutorials session is organized to give conference attendees a comprehensive introduction to a topic of importance drawn from our rapidly growing and changing research field from expert researchers.

This year, as has been the tradition over the past few years, the tutorials committee comprised of tutorials chairs from three conferences: ACL, EMNLP-IJCNLP and NAACL-HLT. A total of 46 tutorial submissions were received, of which 6 were selected for presentation at NAACL-HLT 2019.

The tutorials selected this year are a mix of different topics: from cutting-edge machine learning applied to NLP and emerging applications of NLP to new applications like clinical NLP, to the use of NLP in modeling sociolinguistics and language processing in humans. We hope you find this offering of tutorials compelling, in-depth, instructive and inspiring to your research.

We would like to thank Jill Burstein (NAACL general chair), Nitin Madnani (NAACL website chair), Stephanie Lukin and Alla Roskovskaya (NAACL publications chairs), and Priscilla Rasmussen (local arrangement chair) for their help during the whole process. We also want to extend our sincere gratitude to the other conferences' tutorial chairs who jointly helped with reviewing for all the tutorial submissions: Preslav Nakov and Alexis Palmer (ACL), Tim Baldwin and Marine Carpuat (EMNLP-IJCNLP).

We hope you enjoy the tutorials.

NAACL 2019 Tutorial Co-chairs
Anoop Sarkar
Michael Strube

NAACL HLT Organizers

General Chair

Jill Burstein, Educational Testing Service, USA

Program Co-Chairs:

Christy Doran, Interactions LLC, USA
Thamar Solorio, University of Houston, USA

Tutorials Committee:

Anoop Sarkar, Simon Fraser University, Canada
Michael Strube, Heidelberg Institute for Theoretical Studies, Germany

Table of Contents

Conference Program

Sunday, June 2, 2019

07:30–09:00 *Breakfast*

09:00–12:30 ***Morning Session***

Deep Adversarial Learning for NLP
William Yang Wang, Sameer Singh and Jiwei Li

Deep Learning for Natural Language Inference
Samuel Bowman and Xiaodan Zhu

Measuring and Modeling Language Change
Jacob Eisenstein

10:30–11:00 *Morning Break*

12:30–14:00 *Lunch*

14:00–17:30 ***Afternoon Session***

Transfer Learning in Natural Language Processing
Sebastian Ruder, Matthew E. Peters, Swabha Swayamdipta and Thomas Wolf

Language Learning and Processing in People and Machines
Aida Nematzadeh, Richard Futrell and Roger Levy

Applications of Natural Language Processing in Clinical Research and Practice
Yanshan Wang, Ahmad Tafti, Sunghwan Sohn and Rui Zhang

15:30–16:00 *Afternoon Break*

Sunday, June 2, 2019 (continued)

Deep Adversarial Learning for NLP

William Yang Wang
UC Santa Barbara
william@cs.ucsb.edu

Sameer Singh
UC Irvine
sameer@uci.edu

Jiwei Li
Shannon.ai
jiwei_li@shannonai.com

Abstract

Adversarial learning is a game-theoretic learning paradigm, which has achieved huge successes in the field of Computer Vision recently. It is a general framework that enables a variety of learning models, including the popular Generative Adversarial Networks (GANs). Due to the discrete nature of language, designing adversarial learning models is still challenging for NLP problems.

In this tutorial, we provide a gentle introduction to the foundation of deep adversarial learning, as well as some practical problem formulations and solutions in NLP. We describe recent advances in deep adversarial learning for NLP, with a special focus on generation, adversarial examples & rules, and dialogue. We provide an overview of the research area, categorize different types of adversarial learning models, and discuss pros and cons, aiming to provide some practical perspectives on the future of adversarial learning for solving real-world NLP problems.

1 Tutorial Description

Adversarial learning (AdvL) is an emerging research area that involves a game-theoretical formulation of the learning problem. Recently, with the introduction of Generative Adversarial Networks (GANs) (Goodfellow et al., 2014), we have observed some stunning results in the area of image synthesis in Computer Vision (Brock et al., 2018).

Comparing to images, even language is discrete, the general family of adversarial learning methods still have gained significantly more attentions in NLP in recent years[1]. In contrast to the focus of GANs in Computer Vision, Natural Language Processing researchers have taken a broader approach to adversarial learning. For example, three core technical subareas for adversarial learning include:

- **Adversarial Examples**, where researchers focus on learning or creating adversarial examples or rules to improve the robustness of NLP systems. (Jia and Liang, 2017; Alzantot et al., 2018; Iyyer et al., 2018; Ebrahimi et al., 2018a,b; Shi et al., 2018b; Chen et al., 2018; Farag et al., 2018; Ribeiro et al., 2018; Zhao et al., 2018)
- **Adversarial Training**, which focuses on adding noise, randomness, or adversarial loss during optimization. (Wu et al., 2017; Wang and Bansal, 2018; Li et al., 2018a; Yasunaga et al., 2018; Ponti et al., 2018; Kurita et al., 2018; Kang et al., 2018; Li et al., 2018c; Masumura et al., 2018)
- **Adversarial Generation**, which primarily includes practical solutions of GANs for processing and generation natural language. (Yu et al., 2017; Li et al., 2017; Yang et al., 2018; Wang and Lee, 2018; Xu et al., 2018)

Additionally, we will also introduce other technical focuses such as negative sampling and contrastive estimation (Cai and Wang, 2018; Bose et al., 2018), adversarial evaluation (Elliott, 2018), and reward learning (Wang et al., 2018c). In particular, we will also provide a gentle introduction to the applications of adversarial learning in different NLP problems, including social media (Wang et al., 2018a; Carton et al., 2018), domain adaptation (Kim et al., 2017; Alam et al., 2018; Zou et al., 2018; Chen and Cardie, 2018; Tran and Nguyen, 2018; Cao et al., 2018; Li et al., 2018b), data cleaning (Elazar and Goldberg, 2018; Shah et al., 2018; Ryu et al., 2018; Zellers et al., 2018), information extraction (Qin et al., 2018; Hong et al., 2018; Wang et al., 2018b; Shi et al., 2018a; Bekoulis et al., 2018), and information retrieval (Li and Cheng, 2018).

Adversarial learning methods could easily combine any representation learning based neural networks, and optimize for complex problems in NLP. However, a key challenge for applying deep adversarial learning techniques to real-world sized NLP problems is the model design issue. This tutorial draws connections from theories of deep adversarial learning to practical applications in NLP.

In particular, we start with the gentle introduction to the fundamentals of adversarial learning. We further

[1]Through a simple ACL anthology search, we found that in 2018, there were 20+ times more papers mentioning "adversarial", comparing to 2016. Meanwhile, the growth of all accepted papers is 1.39 times during this period.

Proceedings of NAACL HLT 2019: Tutorial Abstracts, pages 1–5
Minneapolis, Minnesota, June 2, 2019.

discuss their modern deep learning extensions such as Generative Adversarial Networks (Goodfellow et al., 2014). In the first part of the tutorial, we also outline various applications of deep adversarial learning in NLP listed above. In the second part of the tutorial, we will focus on generation of adversarial examples and their uses in NLP tasks, including (1) The inclusion and creation of adversarial examples for robust NLP; (2) The usage of adversarial rules for interpretable and explainable models; and (3) The relationship between adversarial training and adversarial examples. In the third part of the tutorial, we focus on GANs. We start with the general background introduction of generative adversarial learning. We will introduce an in-depth case study of Generative Adversarial Networks for NLP, with a focus on dialogue generation (Li et al., 2017).

This tutorial aims at introducing deep adversarial learning methods to researchers in the NLP community. We do not assume any particular prior knowledge in adversarial learning. The intended length of the tutorial is 3.5 hours, including a coffee break.

2 Outline

Noise-Robust Representation Learning, Adversarial Learning, and Generation are three closely related research subjects in Natural Language Processing. In this tutorial, we touch the intersection of all the three research subjects, covering various aspects of the theories of modern deep adversarial learning methods, and show their successful applications in NLP. This tutorial is organized in three parts:

- **Foundations of Deep Adversarial Learning**. First, we will provide a brief overview of adversarial learning (RL), and discuss the cutting-edge settings in NLP. We describe methods such as Adversarial Training (Wu et al., 2017), Negative Sampling, and Noise Contrastive Estimation (Cai and Wang, 2018; Bose et al., 2018). We introduce domain-adaptation learning approaches, and the widely used data cleaning and information extraction methods (Elazar and Goldberg, 2018; Shah et al., 2018; Ryu et al., 2018; Zellers et al., 2018; Qin et al., 2018; Hong et al., 2018; Wang et al., 2018b; Shi et al., 2018a; Bekoulis et al., 2018). In this part, we also introduce the modern renovation of deep generative adversarial learning (Goodfellow et al., 2014), with a focus on NLP (Yu et al., 2017; Yang et al., 2018; Wang and Lee, 2018; Xu et al., 2018).

- **Adversarial Examples for NLP** Second, we will focus on the designing practical adversarial examples for NLP tasks. In particular, we will provide an overview of recent methods, including their categorization by whether they are white (e.g. Ebrahimi et al., 2018a) or black box (e.g. Iyyer et al., 2018), character- (e.g. Belinkov and Bisk, 2018) or word-based (e.g. Alzantot et al., 2018), and the tasks they have been applied to. We will also provide an in-depth analysis of some of the general techniques for creating adversarial examples, such as gradient-based (e.g. Ebrahimi et al., 2018b), manually-designed (e.g. Jia and Liang, 2017), or learned (e.g. Zhao et al., 2018) perturbation techniques. Next, we will focus on practical applications of adversarial examples, such as existing work on adversarial rules for interpretable NLP (Ribeiro et al., 2018). To conclude this part, we discuss future directions and novel application areas for adversarial examples in NLP, including KB completion (Pezeshkpour et al., 2019).

- **An In-depth Case Study of GANs in NLP.** Third, we switch from the focuses of adversarial training and adversarial examples to generative adversarial networks (Goodfellow et al., 2014). We will discuss why it is challenging to deploy GANs for NLP problems, comparing to vision problems. We then focus on introducing SeqGAN (Yu et al., 2017), an early solution of textual models of GAN, with a focus on policy gradient and Monte Carlo Tree Search. Finally, we provide an in-depth case study of deploying two-agent GAN models for conversational AI (Li et al., 2017). We will summarize the lessons learned, and how we can move forward to investigate game-theoretical approaches in advancing NLP problems.

3 History

The full content of this tutorial has not yet been presented elsewhere, but some parts of this tutorial has also been presented at the following locations in recent years:

1. "*Deep Reinforcement Learning for NLP*", William Wang, Jiwei Li, and Xiaodong He presented at the ACL 2018 Tutorial, Melbourne, AU., Total attendance: 500 (the most popular tutorial).

2. "*Scalable Construction and Reasoning of Massive Knowledge Bases*", Xiang Ren, Nanyun Peng, William Wang. Tutorial at NAACL 2018, New Orleans, Total attendance: 300 (the most popular tutorial).

3. "*Questioning Question Answering Answers*", Sameer Singh, invited talk at the Machine Reading for Question Answering (MRQA) Workshop at ACL 2018 in Melbourne AU, Total attendance: 200 (one of the most popular workshops).

4. "*Teaching a Machine to Converse*", Jiwei Li, presented at OSU, UC Berkeley, UCSB, Harbin Inst. of Technology, total attendance: 500.

5. "*Local, Model-Agnostic Explanations of Machine Learning Predictions*", Sameer Singh, invited

talks and keynotes at various venues, such as UCSD, KAIST, UC Riverside, FICO, and Caltech, total attendance: 800.

4 Duration

The intended duration of this tutorial is 3.5 hours plus a half an hour break.

5 Information About the Presenters

William Wang is an Assistant Professor at the Department of Computer Science, University of California, Santa Barbara. He received his PhD from School of Computer Science, Carnegie Mellon University. He focuses on information extraction and he is the faculty author of KBGAN—the first deep adversarial learning system for knowledge graph reasoning. He has presented tutorials at ACL, NAACL, and IJCAI, with more than 60 published papers at leading conferences and journals including *ACL, EMNLP, NAACL, CVPR, ECCV, COLING, AAAI, IJCAI, CIKM, ICWSM, SIGDIAL, IJCNLP, INTERSPEECH, ICASSP, ASRU, SLT, Machine Learning, and Computer Speech & Language*, and he has received paper awards and honors from CIKM, ASRU, and EMNLP. Website: http://www.cs.ucsb.edu/~william/

Sameer Singh is an Assistant Professor of Computer Science at the University of California, Irvine. He is working on large-scale and interpretable machine learning applied to information extraction and natural language processing. Before UCI, Sameer was a Postdoctoral Research Associate at the University of Washington. He received his PhD from the University of Massachusetts, Amherst in 2014, during which he also interned at Microsoft Research, Google Research, and Yahoo! Labs. His group has received funding from Allen Institute for AI, NSF, Adobe Research, and FICO, and was selected as a DARPA Riser. Sameer has presented tutorials at WSDM and AAAI, and published extensively at top-tier machine learning and natural language processing conferences. Website: http://sameersingh.org/

Jiwei Li is the co-founder and CEO of Shannon.AI, an AI startup based in Beijing, China. He spent three years and received his PhD in Computer Science from Stanford University with Prof. Dan Jurafsky. His research focuses on deep learning in NLP applications, including dialogue, question answering, discourse analysis and information extraction. He has published more than 20 lead-author papers at ACL, EMNLP, NAACL and ICLR, and is the most prolific NLP/ML first author during 2012-2018. He is the lead author of the first study in deep reinforcement learning and adversarial learning for dialogue generation. He is the recipient of a Facebook Fellowship in 2015 and he is named Forbes 30 under 30 in China in 2018. Website: https://nlp.stanford.edu/~bdlijiwei/.

References

Firoj Alam, Shafiq Joty, and Muhammad Imran. 2018. Domain adaptation with adversarial training and graph embeddings. In *Proceedings of the 56th Annual Meeting of the Association for Computational Linguistics (Volume 1: Long Papers)*.

Moustafa Alzantot, Yash Sharma, Ahmed Elgohary, Bo-Jhang Ho, Mani Srivastava, and Kai-Wei Chang. 2018. Generating natural language adversarial examples. *arXiv preprint arXiv:1804.07998*.

Giannis Bekoulis, Johannes Deleu, Thomas Demeester, and Chris Develder. 2018. Adversarial training for multi-context joint entity and relation extraction. In *Proceedings of the 2018 Conference on Empirical Methods in Natural Language Processing*, pages 2830–2836, Brussels, Belgium. Association for Computational Linguistics.

Yonatan Belinkov and Yonatan Bisk. 2018. Synthetic and natural noise both break neural machine translation. In *International Conference on Learning Representations (ICLR)*.

Avishek Bose, Huan Ling, and Yanshuai Cao. 2018. Adversarial contrastive estimation. *ACL*.

Andrew Brock, Jeff Donahue, and Karen Simonyan. 2018. Large scale gan training for high fidelity natural image synthesis. *arXiv preprint arXiv:1809.11096*.

Liwei Cai and William Yang Wang. 2018. Kbgan: Adversarial learning for knowledge graph embeddings. *NAACL*.

Pengfei Cao, Yubo Chen, Kang Liu, Jun Zhao, and Shengping Liu. 2018. Adversarial transfer learning for chinese named entity recognition with self-attention mechanism. In *Proceedings of the 2018 Conference on Empirical Methods in Natural Language Processing*.

Samuel Carton, Qiaozhu Mei, and Paul Resnick. 2018. Extractive adversarial networks: High-recall explanations for identifying personal attacks in social media posts. In *Proceedings of the 2018 Conference on Empirical Methods in Natural Language Processing*.

Hongge Chen, Huan Zhang, Pin-Yu Chen, Jinfeng Yi, and Cho-Jui Hsieh. 2018. Attacking visual language grounding with adversarial examples: A case study on neural image captioning. In *Proceedings of the 56th Annual Meeting of the Association for Computational Linguistics (Volume 1: Long Papers)*.

Xilun Chen and Claire Cardie. 2018. Multinomial adversarial networks for multi-domain text classification. In *Proceedings of the 2018 Conference of the North American Chapter of the Association for Computational Linguistics: Human Language Technologies, Volume 1 (Long Papers)*, volume 1, pages 1226–1240.

Javid Ebrahimi, Daniel Lowd, and Dejing Dou. 2018a. On adversarial examples for character-level neural machine translation. In *Proceedings of the 27th International Conference on Computational Linguistics*, pages 653–663.

Javid Ebrahimi, Anyi Rao, Daniel Lowd, and Dejing Dou. 2018b. Hotflip: White-box adversarial examples for text classification. In *Proceedings of the 56th Annual Meeting of the Association for Computational Linguistics (Volume 2: Short Papers)*, volume 2, pages 31–36.

Yanai Elazar and Yoav Goldberg. 2018. Adversarial removal of demographic attributes from text data. In *Proceedings of the 2018 Conference on Empirical Methods in Natural Language Processing*, pages 11–21.

Desmond Elliott. 2018. Adversarial evaluation of multimodal machine translation. In *Proceedings of the 2018 Conference on Empirical Methods in Natural Language Processing*, pages 2974–2978.

Youmna Farag, Helen Yannakoudakis, and Ted Briscoe. 2018. Neural automated essay scoring and coherence modeling for adversarially crafted input. In *Proceedings of the 2018 Conference of the North American Chapter of the Association for Computational Linguistics: Human Language Technologies, Volume 1 (Long Papers)*.

Ian Goodfellow, Jean Pouget-Abadie, Mehdi Mirza, Bing Xu, David Warde-Farley, Sherjil Ozair, Aaron Courville, and Yoshua Bengio. 2014. Generative adversarial nets. In *Advances in neural information processing systems*, pages 2672–2680.

Yu Hong, Wenxuan Zhou, jingli zhang, Guodong Zhou, and Qiaoming Zhu. 2018. Self-regulation: Employing a generative adversarial network to improve event detection. In *Proceedings of the 56th Annual Meeting of the Association for Computational Linguistics (Volume 1: Long Papers)*.

Mohit Iyyer, John Wieting, Kevin Gimpel, and Luke Zettlemoyer. 2018. Adversarial example generation with syntactically controlled paraphrase networks. In *Proceedings of NAACL-HLT*, pages 1875–1885.

Robin Jia and Percy Liang. 2017. Adversarial examples for evaluating reading comprehension systems. In *Proceedings of the 2017 Conference on Empirical Methods in Natural Language Processing*, pages 2021–2031.

Dongyeop Kang, Tushar Khot, Ashish Sabharwal, and Eduard Hovy. 2018. Adventure: Adversarial training for textual entailment with knowledge-guided examples. In *Proceedings of the 56th Annual Meeting of the Association for Computational Linguistics (Volume 1: Long Papers)*.

Young-Bum Kim, Karl Stratos, and Dongchan Kim. 2017. Adversarial adaptation of synthetic or stale data. In *Proceedings of the 55th Annual Meeting of the Association for Computational Linguistics (Volume 1: Long Papers)*, volume 1, pages 1297–1307.

Shuhei Kurita, Daisuke Kawahara, and Sadao Kurohashi. 2018. Neural adversarial training for semi-supervised japanese predicate-argument structure analysis. In *Proceedings of the 56th Annual Meeting of the Association for Computational Linguistics (Volume 1: Long Papers)*.

Bo Li and Ping Cheng. 2018. Learning neural representation for clir with adversarial framework. In *Proceedings of the 2018 Conference on Empirical Methods in Natural Language Processing*, pages 1861–1870.

Jiwei Li, Will Monroe, Tianlin Shi, Sébastien Jean, Alan Ritter, and Dan Jurafsky. 2017. Adversarial learning for neural dialogue generation. *EMNLP*.

Juntao Li, Yan Song, Haisong Zhang, Dongmin Chen, Shuming Shi, Dongyan Zhao, and Rui Yan. 2018a. Generating classical chinese poems via conditional variational autoencoder and adversarial training. In *Proceedings of the 2018 Conference on Empirical Methods in Natural Language Processing*.

Yitong Li, Timothy Baldwin, and Trevor Cohn. 2018b. What's in a domain? learning domain-robust text representations using adversarial training. In *Proceedings of the 2018 Conference of the North American Chapter of the Association for Computational Linguistics: Human Language Technologies, Volume 2 (Short Papers)*.

Zhongyang Li, Xiao Ding, and Ting Liu. 2018c. Generating reasonable and diversified story ending using sequence to sequence model with adversarial training. In *Proceedings of the 27th International Conference on Computational Linguistics*.

Ryo Masumura, Yusuke Shinohara, Ryuichiro Higashinaka, and Yushi Aono. 2018. Adversarial training for multi-task and multi-lingual joint modeling of utterance intent classification. In *Proceedings of the 2018 Conference on Empirical Methods in Natural Language Processing*.

Pouya Pezeshkpour, Yifan Tian, and Sameer Singh. 2019. Investigating robustness and interpretability of link prediction via adversarial modifications. In *Annual Conference of the North American Chapter of the Association for Computational Linguistics (NAACL)*.

Edoardo Maria Ponti, Ivan Vulić, Goran Glavaš, Nikola Mrkšić, and Anna Korhonen. 2018. Adversarial propagation and zero-shot cross-lingual transfer of word vector specialization. In *Proceedings of the 2018 Conference on Empirical Methods in Natural Language Processing*.

Pengda Qin, Weiran Xu, and William Yang Wang. 2018. Dsgan: Generative adversarial training for robust distant supervision relation extraction. In *Proceedings of the 56th Annual Meeting of the Association for Computational Linguistics*, Melbourne, Victoria, Australia. ACL.

Marco Tulio Ribeiro, Sameer Singh, and Carlos Guestrin. 2018. Semantically equivalent adversarial rules for debugging nlp models. In *Proceedings of the 56th Annual Meeting of the Association for Computational Linguistics (Volume 1: Long Papers)*, volume 1, pages 856–865.

Seonghan Ryu, Sangjun Koo, Hwanjo Yu, and Gary Geunbae Lee. 2018. Out-of-domain detection based on generative adversarial network. In *Proceedings of the 2018 Conference on Empirical Methods in Natural Language Processing*, pages 714–718.

Darsh Shah, Tao Lei, Alessandro Moschitti, Salvatore Romeo, and Preslav Nakov. 2018. Adversarial domain adaptation for duplicate question detection. In *Proceedings of the 2018 Conference on Empirical Methods in Natural Language Processing*, pages 1056–1063.

Ge Shi, Chong Feng, Lifu Huang, Boliang Zhang, Heng Ji, Lejian Liao, and Heyan Huang. 2018a. Genre separation network with adversarial training for cross-genre relation extraction. In *Proceedings of the 2018 Conference on Empirical Methods in Natural Language Processing*.

Haoyue Shi, Jiayuan Mao, Tete Xiao, Yuning Jiang, and Jian Sun. 2018b. Learning visually-grounded semantics from contrastive adversarial samples. In *Proceedings of the 27th International Conference on Computational Linguistics*.

Van-Khanh Tran and Le-Minh Nguyen. 2018. Adversarial domain adaptation for variational neural language generation in dialogue systems. In *Proceedings of the 27th International Conference on Computational Linguistics*, pages 1205–1217.

Weichao Wang, Shi Feng, Wei Gao, Daling Wang, and Yifei Zhang. 2018a. Personalized microblog sentiment classification via adversarial cross-lingual multi-task learning. In *Proceedings of the 2018 Conference on Empirical Methods in Natural Language Processing*.

Xiaozhi Wang, Xu Han, Yankai Lin, Zhiyuan Liu, and Maosong Sun. 2018b. Adversarial multi-lingual neural relation extraction. In *Proceedings of the 27th International Conference on Computational Linguistics*, pages 1156–1166.

Xin Wang, Wenhu Chen, Yuan-Fang Wang, and William Yang Wang. 2018c. No metrics are perfect: Adversarial reward learning for visual storytelling. In *ACL*.

Yaushian Wang and Hung-yi Lee. 2018. Learning to encode text as human-readable summaries using generative adversarial networks. In *Proceedings of the 2018 Conference on Empirical Methods in Natural Language Processing*.

Yicheng Wang and Mohit Bansal. 2018. Robust machine comprehension models via adversarial training. In *Proceedings of the 2018 Conference of the North American Chapter of the Association for Computational Linguistics: Human Language Technologies, Volume 2 (Short Papers)*, volume 2, pages 575–581.

Yi Wu, David Bamman, and Stuart Russell. 2017. Adversarial training for relation extraction. In *Proceedings of the 2017 Conference on Empirical Methods in Natural Language Processing*, pages 1778–1783.

Jingjing Xu, Xuancheng Ren, Junyang Lin, and Xu Sun. 2018. Diversity-promoting gan: A cross-entropy based generative adversarial network for diversified text generation. In *Proceedings of the 2018 Conference on Empirical Methods in Natural Language Processing*.

Zhen Yang, Wei Chen, Feng Wang, and Bo Xu. 2018. Improving neural machine translation with conditional sequence generative adversarial nets. In *Proceedings of the 2018 Conference of the North American Chapter of the Association for Computational Linguistics: Human Language Technologies, Volume 1 (Long Papers)*.

Michihiro Yasunaga, Jungo Kasai, and Dragomir Radev. 2018. Robust multilingual part-of-speech tagging via adversarial training. In *Proceedings of the 2018 Conference of the North American Chapter of the Association for Computational Linguistics: Human Language Technologies, Volume 1 (Long Papers)*.

Lantao Yu, Weinan Zhang, Jun Wang, and Yong Yu. 2017. Seqgan: Sequence generative adversarial nets with policy gradient. *AAAI*.

Rowan Zellers, Yonatan Bisk, Roy Schwartz, and Yejin Choi. 2018. Swag: A large-scale adversarial dataset for grounded commonsense inference. In *Proceedings of the 2018 Conference on Empirical Methods in Natural Language Processing*.

Zhengli Zhao, Dheeru Dua, and Sameer Singh. 2018. Generating natural adversarial examples. In *International Conference on Learning Representations (ICLR)*.

Bowei Zou, Zengzhuang Xu, Yu Hong, and Guodong Zhou. 2018. Adversarial feature adaptation for cross-lingual relation classification. In *Proceedings of the 27th International Conference on Computational Linguistics*, pages 437–448.

Deep Learning for Natural Language Inference

Samuel R. Bowman
New York University
bowman@nyu.edu

Xiaodan Zhu
ECE, Queen's University
zhu2048@gmail.com

1 Description

The task of natural language inference (NLI; also known as recognizing textual entailment, or RTE) asks a system to evaluate the relationships between the truth-conditional meanings of two sentences or, in other words, decide whether one sentence follows from another. This task neatly isolates the core NLP problem of sentence understanding as a classification problem, and also offers promise as an intermediate step in the building of complex systems (Dagan et al., 2005; MacCartney, 2009; Bowman et al., 2015).

The last few years have seen fast progress in NLI, with the introduction of a few large training datasets and many popular evaluation sets as well as an explosion of new model architectures and methods for using unlabeled data and outside knowledge. This tutorial will layout the motivations for work on NLI, survey the available resources for the task, and present highlights from recent research showing us what NLI can teach us about the capabilities and limits of deep learning models for language understanding and reasoning.

The tutorial will start from a brief discussion on the motivations for NLI, problem definitions, and typical conventional approaches (Dagan et al., 2013; MacCartney, 2009; Iftene and Balahur-Dobrescu, 2007).

Critical to the recent advance on NLI, the creation of larger annotated datasets (Bowman et al., 2015; Williams et al., 2018; Conneau et al., 2018) has made it feasible to train complex models that need to estimate a large number of parameters. The tutorial will present detailed discussion on the available datasets as well as the motivations for and insights from developing these datasets. Then based on more recent research on annotation artifacts, we will extend the discussion to what we should or shouldn't take away from the current datasets.

We will then focus on the cutting-edge deep learning models for NLI. We start from two basic setups for NLI modeling: sentence-embedding-based modeling (Bowman et al., 2015; Chen et al., 2017b, 2018a; Williams et al., 2018; Yoon et al., 2018; Kiela et al., 2018; Talman et al., 2018) and deep-learning approaches that utilize cross-sentence statistics (Bowman et al., 2015; Chen et al., 2017a, 2018b; Radford et al., 2018; Devlin et al., 2018; Peters et al., 2018). We will cover typical deep-learning architectures in both paradigms.

Based on this we will deepen our discussion from several perspectives. We first describe models that can further consider linguistic structures in the deep-learning NLI architectures (Chen et al., 2017a). We then advance to discuss models that utilize external knowledge, which include two typical types of approaches: those explicitly incorporating human-authorized knowledge (Chen et al., 2018b) and those based on unsupervised pretraining (Radford et al., 2018; Devlin et al., 2018; Peters et al., 2018). We will present how NLI models are sensitive or robust to different newly proposed tests (Glockner et al., 2018; Wang et al., 2018; Naik et al., 2018; Poliak et al., 2018). The tutorial will also cover the recent modeling on cross-lingual NLI (Conneau et al., 2018).

Finally we will summarize the tutorial and flesh out some discussions on future directions.

2 Tutorial Outline

- Introduction
- Background
  - Problem definition
  - Motivations
- History and conventional methods
  - Natural logic methods
  - Theorem proving methods
- Recent advance on dataset development
  - Motivations
  - Detailed discussions/insights on dataset development and available datasets
  - Recent research on annotation artifacts representation
- Cutting-edge deep learning models

Proceedings of NAACL HLT 2019: Tutorial Abstracts, pages 6–8
Minneapolis, Minnesota, June 2, 2019.

- ◦ Sentence-embedding-based models
  - ◦ Deep learning architectures exploring cross-sentence statistics
  - ◦ Models enhanced with linguistic structures
  - ◦ Modeling external knowledge
  - ◦ Recent advance on pretrain-based models
  - ◦ Cross-lingual NLI Models
  - ◦ Revisiting data and model limitation jointly
- Applications
  - ◦ Existing and potential downstream applications
    - ▪ MNLI for evaluation
    - ▪ MNLI for pretraining (incl. RTE)
  - ◦ NLI for evaluating sentence representation
- Summary

3 Instructors

Sam Bowman, New York University.
bowman@nyu.edu
`http://www.nyu.edu/projects/bowman`

Sam Bowman is an Assistant Professor of Data Science and Linguistics at New York University. Sam works on building artificial neural network models for sentence understanding, with the dual goals of both improving language technology for problems like translation and facilitating basic research on human language. He co-directs the Machine Learning for Language group (with Prof. Kyunghyun Cho) and the larger CILVR applied machine learning lab. He completed a PhD at Stanford University in 2016 with advisors Chris Manning and Chris Potts. He received a 2017 Google Faculty Research Award and led a twenty-researcher team project during the summer of 2018 as part of the JSALT workshop program.

Xiaodan Zhu, Queen's University, Canada.
zhu2048@gmail.com
`http://www.xiaodanzhu.com`

Xiaodan Zhu is an Assistant Professor of the Department of Electrical and Computer Engineering of Queen's University, Canada. His research interests are in natural language processing and machine learning. His recent work has focused on natural language inference, sentiment analysis, semantic composition, and summarization. He has presented tutorials before at ACL-2017 and EMNLP-2014.

References

Samuel R. Bowman, Gabor Angeli, Christopher Potts, and Christopher D. Manning. 2015. A large annotated corpus for learning natural language inference. In *EMNLP*.

Qian Chen, Zhen-Hua Ling, and Xiaodan Zhu. 2018a. Enhancing sentence embedding with generalized pooling. In *COLING*.

Qian Chen, Xiaodan Zhu, Zhen-Hua Ling, Diana Inkpen, and Si Wei. 2018b. Neural natural language inference models enhanced with external knowledge. In *ACL*.

Qian Chen, Xiaodan Zhu, Zhen-Hua Ling, Si Wei, Hui Jiang, and Diana Inkpen. 2017a. Enhanced lstm for natural language inference. In *ACL*.

Qian Chen, Xiaodan Zhu, Zhen-Hua Ling, Si Wei, Hui Jiang, and Diana Inkpen. 2017b. Recurrent neural network-based sentence encoder with gated attention for natural language inference. In *EMNLP RepEval Workshop*.

Alexis Conneau, Ruty Rinott, Guillaume Lample, Adina Williams, Samuel R. Bowman, Holger Schwenk, and Veselin Stoyanov. 2018. Xnli: Evaluating cross-lingual sentence representations. In *EMNLP*.

Ido Dagan, Oren Glickman, and Bernardo Magnini. 2005. The PASCAL recognising textual entailment challenge. In *MLCW*.

Ido Dagan, Dan Roth, Mark Sammons, and Fabio Massimo Zanzotto. 2013. *Recognizing Textual Entailment: Models and Applications*. Synthesis Lectures on Human Language Technologies. Morgan Claypool Publishers.

Jacob Devlin, Ming-Wei Chang, Kenton Lee, and Kristina Toutanova. 2018. Bert: Pre-training of deep bidirectional transformers for language understanding. *arXiv preprint arXiv:1810.04805* .

Max Glockner, Vered Shwartz, and Yoav Goldberg. 2018. Breaking nli systems with sentences that require simple lexical inferences. *arXiv preprint arXiv: 1805.02266* .

Adrian Iftene and Alexandra Balahur-Dobrescu. 2007. *Proceedings of the ACL-PASCAL Workshop on Textual Entailment and Paraphrasing*.

Douwe Kiela, Changhan Wang, and Kyunghyun Cho. 2018. Dynamic meta-embeddings for improved sentence representations. *arXiv preprint arXiv: 1804.07983* .

Bill MacCartney. 2009. *Natural Language Inference*. Ph.D. thesis, Stanford University.

Aakanksha Naik, Abhilasha Ravichander, Norman Sadeh, Carolyn Rose, and Graham Neubig. 2018. Stress test evaluation for natural language inference. *arXiv preprint arXiv:1806.00692* .

Matthew E Peters, Mark Neumann, Mohit Iyyer, Matt Gardner, Christopher Clark, Kenton Lee, and Luke Zettlemoyer. 2018. Deep contextualized word representations. *arXiv preprint arXiv:1802.05365* .

Adam Poliak, Jason Naradowsky, Aparajita Haldar, Rachel Rudinger, and Benjamin Van Durme. 2018. Hypothesis only baselines in natural language inference. *arXiv preprint arXiv: 1805.01042* .

Alec Radford, Karthik Narasimhan, Tim Salimans, and Ilya Sutskever. 2018. Improving language understanding by generative pre-training. *Technical Report, OpenAI* .

Aarne Talman, Anssi Yli-Jyrä, and Jörg Tiedemann. 2018. Natural language inference with hierarchical bilstm max pooling architecture. *arXiv preprint arXiv:1808.08762* .

Haohan Wang, Da Sun, and Eric P. Xing. 2018. What if we simply swap the two text fragments? a straightforward yet effective way to test the robustness of methods to confounding signals in nature language inference tasks. *arXiv preprint arXiv: 1809.02719* .

Adina Williams, Nikita Nangia, and Samuel Bowman. 2018. A broad-coverage challenge corpus for sentence understanding through inference. In *NAACL*.

Deunsol Yoon, Dongbok Lee, and SangKeun Lee. 2018. Dynamic self-attention: Computing attention over words dynamically for sentence embedding. *arXiv preprint arXiv: 1808.07383* .

Measuring and Modeling Language Change

Jacob Eisenstein
Georgia Institute of Technology and Facebook Artificial Intelligence Research
me@jacob-eisenstein.com

1 Description

This tutorial is designed to help researchers answer the following sorts of questions about how language usage varies over time:

- Are people happier on the weekend?
- What was 1861's word of the year?
- Are Democrats and Republicans more different than ever?
- When did "gay" stop meaning "happy"?
- Are gender stereotypes getting weaker, stronger, or just different?
- Who is a leader, and who is a follower?
- How can we get internet users to be more polite and objective?

Such questions are fundamental to the social sciences and humanities, and scholars in these disciplines are turning to computational techniques for answers (e.g., Evans and Aceves, 2016; Underwood et al., 2018; Barron et al., 2018). Meanwhile, the ACL community is increasingly engaged with data that varies across time (e.g., Rayson et al., 2007; Yang and Eisenstein, 2016), and with the social insights that can be offered by analyzing temporal patterns and trends (e.g., Tsur et al., 2015). The purpose of this tutorial is to facilitate this convergence in two main ways.

First, by synthesizing recent computational techniques for handling and modeling temporal data, such as dynamic word embeddings, the tutorial will provide a starting point for future computational research. It will also identify useful text analytic tools for social scientists and digital humanities scholars, such as dynamic topic models and dynamic word embeddings.

Second, the tutorial will provide an overview of techniques and datasets from the quantitative social sciences and the digital humanities, which are not well-known in the computational linguistics community. These techniques include hypothesis testing, survival analysis, Hawkes processes, and causal inference. Datasets include historical newspaper archives, social media, and corpora of contemporary political speech.

1.1 Format

The format of this three-hour tutorial will combine lecture-style surveys of various research areas with interactive coding demonstrations. The coding demonstrations will use Jupyter notebook and the numpy, scipy, and pandas libraries. These notebooks will be shared along with publicly available data in a github repository for the tutorial.[1]

1.2 Scope

This tutorial is focused on **corpus-based** methods for measuring and modeling changes in language usage from time-stamped documents. Another body of research is built on **type-level** resources, such as lists of aligned words across languages, which can support phylogenetic analysis of language history (e.g. Gray and Atkinson, 2003; Bouchard-Côté et al., 2013). Other researchers use **simulation** to test the consequences of theoretical models of language change (e.g. Niyogi and Berwick, 1997; Cotterell et al., 2018). Finally, sociolinguists make use of **apparent time**, a technique for measuring language change by comparing the speech of individuals of various ages (e.g., Tagliamonte and D'Arcy, 2009). These three methods all contribute to our overall understanding of language change, but in the interest of a compact and coherent presentation, this tutorial will focus exclusively on corpus-based techniques.

[1] https://github.com/jacobeisenstein/language-change-tutorial

Proceedings of NAACL HLT 2019: Tutorial Abstracts, pages 9–14
Minneapolis, Minnesota, June 2, 2019.

The tutorial will engage with statistical analysis (e.g., hypothesis testing, causal inference) to a greater extent than most NAACL papers. Every effort will be made to make this material accessible to the typical NAACL attendee.

2 Topics

The bulk of the tutorial consists of hands-on exploration of time-stamped textual data, which will be conducted in the form of Jupyter notebooks. These practical sessions will be book-ended by an introduction to theoretical and methodological perspectives on language change, and a brief discussion of open questions for future work.

2.1 How and why to measure language change?

The tutorial begins with a survey of theoretical questions and associated methodological approaches. Sociolinguists and historical linguists are interested in changes to the linguistic system (Weinreich et al., 1968; Pierrehumbert, 2010); digital humanists model changes in text over time to track the evolution of cultural and literary practices (Michel et al., 2011); computational social scientists use time-stamped corpora to understand the transmission and evolution of social practices (Kooti et al., 2012; Garg et al., 2018) and to identify causes and effects in social systems (Bernal et al., 2017; Chandrasekharan et al., 2018). We will survey some of the ways in which various disciplines approach language change, and briefly discuss alternatives to the corpus-based perspective taken in this tutorial.

2.2 Tracking changes in word frequency

Question: Are people happier on the weekend?

Data: Twitter sentiment (Golder and Macy, 2011)

Methods: hypothesis testing, regression, python dataframes

In a seminal paper in social media analysis, Golder and Macy (2011) use Twitter data to quantify sentiment by time-of-day and day-of-the-week. This provides an opportunity to apply fundamental methods in quantitative social science to a time-stamped corpus of text, while gaining familiarity with the python data science stack. We will replicate the results of Golder and Macy, and then extend them, exploring Simpson's paradox and questions of representativeness (Biber, 1993; Pechenick et al., 2015).

2.3 Quantifying differences over time

Question: Are Democrats and Republicans more polarized than ever?

Data: Legislative floor speeches (Gentzkow et al., 2016)

Methods: topic models, information theory, randomization

Many observers have concluded that American politicians are increasingly polarized. Voting records are the main empirical foundation for this claim (e.g., Bateman et al., 2016), but legislative votes may be taken for non-ideological reasons, such as party discipline (Peterson and Spirling, 2018). Text analysis has therefore been proposed as a technique for quantifying ideological differences across groups, via either individual word frequencies (Monroe et al., 2008; Gentzkow et al., 2016) or latent topics (Tsur et al., 2015; Barron et al., 2018). Similar techniques can be used to track similarity and difference across literary genres (Underwood et al., 2018), academic conferences (Hall et al., 2008), and social media communities (Danescu-Niculescu-Mizil et al., 2013). In this section, we will apply language models, topic models, and information theory to a dataset of legislative speech, quantifying the textual distance between U.S. political parties over time.

2.4 Detecting changes in meaning

Question: When did money become something you can launder?

Data: Legal opinions from `courtlistener.com`

Methods: dynamic word embeddings

Word embeddings capture lexical semantics in vector form, but word meaning can change over time through a variety of linguistic mechanisms (Tahmasebi et al., 2018). This section will survey methods for computing *diachronic* word embeddings, which are parameterized by time (Wijaya and Yeniterzi, 2011; Kulkarni et al., 2015; Hamilton et al., 2016; Garg et al., 2018; Rudolph and Blei, 2018; Rosenfeld and Erk, 2018). We will investigate the application of one such method to a corpus of historical texts, identifying words with particularly fluid semantics, and teasing apart these different meanings.

2.5 Distinguishing leaders and followers

Question: Who is setting the terms of the debate?

Data: 2012 Republican primary debates (Nguyen et al., 2014)

Methods: Granger causation, Hawkes Process

Language changes have leaders and followers, and there is considerable interest in identifying the specific individuals and types of individuals who drive change (Dietz et al., 2007; Gerrish and Blei, 2010; Kooti et al., 2012; Eisenstein et al., 2014; Goel et al., 2016; Gerow et al., 2018; Del Tredici and Fernández, 2018). We will explore data from the 2012 Republican primary debates (Nguyen et al., 2014), applying a Hawkes process model to try to identify individuals whose language most shaped the terms of the debate. This section will also cover epidemiological models that attempt to predict *who* will be affected next in a cascade, and to quantify the factors that make an individual more or less susceptible (Soni et al., 2018).

2.6 Predicting the future

Question: Which innovations will persist?

Data: Reddit neologisms (Stewart and Eisenstein, 2018)

Methods: survival analysis

Some changes pass the test of time, but others are ephemera (Dury and Drouin, 2009). Is it possible to predict what will happen in advance? By attacking this problem, we hope to better understand the social and linguistic mechanisms that underlie language change (Chesley and Baayen, 2010; Del Tredici and Fernández, 2018; Stewart and Eisenstein, 2018). The dataset for this evaluation will consist of a set of lexical innovations from Reddit. We will build models to predict not only which will survive, but for how long.

2.7 Causation and the arrow of time

Question: Can internet policies make people be nicer?

Data: Counts of hate speech lexicons on Reddit (Chandrasekharan et al., 2018)

Methods: interrupted time series

Because causes precede effects, it is natural to ask whether temporal data can support causal inferences. This section will begin by reviewing the potential outcomes framework, which is the classical approach to causal inference from observational data (Rosenbaum, 2017). This framework is based on three main concepts: *treatment* (the manipulation of the environment whose effect we want to test), *outcome* (the quantity to measure), and *confounds* (additional variables that are probabilistically associated with both the treatment and effect). We will discuss how the potential outcomes framework can apply to temporal data through the interrupted time series model (Bernal et al., 2017), and we will experiment with the impact of a discrete policy treatment on textual outcomes in social media (Chandrasekharan et al., 2018; Pavalanathan et al., 2018). This section will also briefly survey approaches to modeling text as a treatment (Fong and Grimmer, 2016; Egami et al., 2018).

2.8 What's next?

We will conclude with a discussion of open research questions for the analysis of language change and diachronic textual corpora (Nerbonne, 2010; Eisenstein, 2013; Maurits and Griffiths, 2014; Perek, 2014).

3 Presenter

Jacob Eisenstein is Associate Professor in the School of Interactive Computing at the Georgia Institute of Technology, which he joined in 2012. He is on sabbatical at Facebook Artificial Intelligence Research in Seattle. His research on computational sociolinguistics is supported by an NSF CAREER award and by a young investigator award from the Air Force Office of Scientific Research (AFOSR). Results from this research have been published in traditional natural language processing venues, in sociolinguistics journals, and in more general venues. Jacob's Georgia Tech course on Computational Social Science covers some of the same themes as this tutorial, and includes some additional material.[2] He recently completed an introductory textbook on natural language processing.

References

Alexander TJ Barron, Jenny Huang, Rebecca L Spang, and Simon DeDeo. 2018. Individuals, institutions, and innovation in the debates of the french revolution. *Proceedings of the National Academy of Sciences*, 115(18):4607–4612.

David A. Bateman, Joshua D. Clinton, and John S. Lapinski. 2016. A house divided? roll calls, po-

[2] https://github.com/jacobeisenstein/gt-css-class

larization, and policy differences in the u.s. house, 1877–2011. 61:698–714.

James Lopez Bernal, Steven Cummins, and Antonio Gasparrini. 2017. Interrupted time series regression for the evaluation of public health interventions: a tutorial. *International journal of epidemiology*, 46(1):348–355.

Douglas Biber. 1993. Representativeness in corpus design. *Literary and linguistic computing*, 8(4):243–257.

Alexandre Bouchard-Côté, David Hall, Thomas L Griffiths, and Dan Klein. 2013. Automated reconstruction of ancient languages using probabilistic models of sound change. *Proceedings of the National Academy of Sciences*, page 201204678.

Eshwar Chandrasekharan, Umashanthi Pavalanathan, Anirudh Srinivasan, Adam Glynn, Jacob Eisenstein, and Eric Gilbert. 2018. You can't stay here: The effectiveness of Reddit's 2015 ban through the lens of hate speech. In *Proceedings of Computer-Supported Cooperative Work (CSCW)*.

Paula Chesley and R Harald Baayen. 2010. Predicting new words from newer words: Lexical borrowings in french. *Linguistics*, 48(6).

Ryan Cotterell, Christo Kirov, Mans Hulden, and Jason Eisner. 2018. On the diachronic stability of irregularity in inflectional morphology. *arXiv preprint arXiv:1804.08262*.

Cristian Danescu-Niculescu-Mizil, Robert West, Dan Jurafsky, Jure Leskovec, and Christopher Potts. 2013. No country for old members: User lifecycle and linguistic change in online communities. In *Proceedings of the Conference on World-Wide Web (WWW)*, pages 307–318.

Marco Del Tredici and Raquel Fernández. 2018. The road to success: Assessing the fate of linguistic innovations in online communities. In *Proceedings of the International Conference on Computational Linguistics (COLING)*, pages 1591–1603.

Laura Dietz, Steffen Bickel, and Tobias Scheffer. 2007. Unsupervised prediction of citation influences. In *Proceedings of the 24th international conference on Machine learning*, pages 233–240. ACM.

Pascaline Dury and Patrick Drouin. 2009. When terms disappear from a specialized lexicon: A semi-automatic investigation into necrology. In *Actes de la conférence internationale" Language for Special Purposes"(LSP 2009)*.

Naoki Egami, Christian J Fong, Justin Grimmer, Margaret E Roberts, and Brandon M Stewart. 2018. How to make causal inferences using texts. *arXiv preprint arXiv:1802.02163*.

Jacob Eisenstein. 2013. What to do about bad language on the internet. In *Proceedings of the North American Chapter of the Association for Computational Linguistics (NAACL)*, pages 359–369.

Jacob Eisenstein, Brendan O'Connor, Noah A. Smith, and Eric P. Xing. 2014. Diffusion of lexical change in social media. *PLoS ONE*, 9.

James A Evans and Pedro Aceves. 2016. Machine translation: mining text for social theory. *Annual Review of Sociology*, 42.

Christian Fong and Justin Grimmer. 2016. Discovery of treatments from text corpora. In *Proceedings of the Association for Computational Linguistics (ACL)*, pages 1600–1609.

Nikhil Garg, Londa Schiebinger, Dan Jurafsky, and James Zou. 2018. Word embeddings quantify 100 years of gender and ethnic stereotypes. *Proceedings of the National Academy of Sciences*, 115(16):E3635–E3644.

Matthew Gentzkow, Jesse Shapiro, and Matt Taddy. 2016. Measuring polarization in high-dimensional data: Method and application to congressional speech. Technical Report 22423, NBER Working Papers.

Aaron Gerow, Yuening Hu, Jordan Boyd-Graber, David M Blei, and James A Evans. 2018. Measuring discursive influence across scholarship. *Proceedings of the National Academy of Sciences*, page 201719792.

Sean Gerrish and David M Blei. 2010. A language-based approach to measuring scholarly impact. In *Proceedings of the International Conference on Machine Learning (ICML)*, pages 375–382.

Rahul Goel, Sandeep Soni, Naman Goyal, John Paparrizos, Hanna Wallach, Fernando Diaz, and Jacob Eisenstein. 2016. The social dynamics of language change in online networks. In *The International Conference on Social Informatics (SocInfo)*.

Scott A Golder and Michael W Macy. 2011. Diurnal and seasonal mood vary with work, sleep, and daylength across diverse cultures. *Science*, 333(6051):1878–1881.

Russell D Gray and Quentin D Atkinson. 2003. Language-tree divergence times support the anatolian theory of indo-european origin. *Nature*, 426(6965):435.

David Hall, Daniel Jurafsky, and Christopher D Manning. 2008. Studying the history of ideas using topic models. In *Proceedings of Empirical Methods for Natural Language Processing (EMNLP)*, pages 363–371.

William L Hamilton, Jure Leskovec, and Dan Jurafsky. 2016. Diachronic word embeddings reveal statistical laws of semantic change. In *Proceedings of the Association for Computational Linguistics (ACL)*.

Farshad Kooti, Haeryun Yang, Meeyoung Cha, P. Krishna Gummadi, and Winter A Mason. 2012. The emergence of conventions in online social networks. In *Proceedings of the International Conference on Web and Social Media (ICWSM)*, pages 194–201.

Vivek Kulkarni, Rami Al-Rfou, Bryan Perozzi, and Steven Skiena. 2015. Statistically significant detection of linguistic change. In *Proceedings of the Conference on World-Wide Web (WWW)*, pages 625–635.

Luke Maurits and Thomas L Griffiths. 2014. Tracing the roots of syntax with bayesian phylogenetics. *Proceedings of the National Academy of Sciences*, 111(37):13576–13581.

Jean-Baptiste Michel, Yuan Kui Shen, Aviva Presser Aiden, Adrian Veres, Matthew K Gray, Joseph P Pickett, Dale Hoiberg, Dan Clancy, Peter Norvig, Jon Orwant, et al. 2011. Quantitative analysis of culture using millions of digitized books. *science*, 331(6014):176–182.

Burt L. Monroe, Michael P. Colaresi, and Kevin M. Quinn. 2008. Fightin'words: Lexical feature selection and evaluation for identifying the content of political conflict. *Political Analysis*, 16(4):372–403.

John Nerbonne. 2010. Measuring the diffusion of linguistic change. *Philosophical Transactions of the Royal Society of London B: Biological Sciences*, 365(1559):3821–3828.

Viet-An Nguyen, Jordan Boyd-Graber, Philip Resnik, Deborah A Cai, Jennifer E Midberry, and Yuanxin Wang. 2014. Modeling topic control to detect influence in conversations using nonparametric topic models. *Machine Learning*, 95(3):381–421.

Partha Niyogi and Robert C. Berwick. 1997. A dynamical systems model for language change. *Complex Systems*, 11(3):161–204.

Umashanthi Pavalanathan, Xiaochuang Han, and Jacob Eisenstein. 2018. Mind your POV: Convergence of articles and editors towards wikipedia's neutrality norm. In *Proceedings of Computer-Supported Cooperative Work (CSCW)*.

Eitan Adam Pechenick, Christopher M Danforth, and Peter Sheridan Dodds. 2015. Characterizing the google books corpus: Strong limits to inferences of socio-cultural and linguistic evolution. *PloS one*, 10(10):e0137041.

Florent Perek. 2014. Vector spaces for historical linguistics: Using distributional semantics to study syntactic productivity in diachrony. In *Proceedings of the 52nd Annual Meeting of the Association for Computational Linguistics (Volume 2: Short Papers)*, volume 2, pages 309–314.

Andrew Peterson and Arthur Spirling. 2018. Classification accuracy as a substantive quantity of interest: Measuring polarization in westminster systems. *Political Analysis*, 26(1):120–128.

Janet B. Pierrehumbert. 2010. The dynamic lexicon. In A. Cohn, M. Huffman, and C. Fougeron, editors, *Handbook of Laboratory Phonology*, pages 173–183. Oxford University Press.

Paul Rayson, Dawn Archer, Alistair Baron, Jonathan Culpeper, and Nicholas Smith. 2007. Tagging the bard: Evaluating the accuracy of a modern pos tagger on early modern english corpora. In *Corpus Linguistics Conference*.

Paul R Rosenbaum. 2017. *Observation and experiment: an introduction to causal inference*. Harvard University Press.

Alex Rosenfeld and Katrin Erk. 2018. Deep neural models of semantic shift. In *Proceedings of the North American Chapter of the Association for Computational Linguistics (NAACL)*, pages 474–484.

Maja Rudolph and David Blei. 2018. Dynamic embeddings for language evolution. In *Proceedings of the 2018 World Wide Web Conference on World Wide Web*, pages 1003–1011. International World Wide Web Conferences Steering Committee.

Sandeep Soni, Shawn Ling Ramirez, and Jacob Eisenstein. 2018. Discriminative modeling of social influence for prediction and explanation in event cascades. *arXiv preprint arXiv:1802.06138*.

Ian Stewart and Jacob Eisenstein. 2018. Making "fetch" happen: The influence of social and linguistic context on the success of lexical innovations. In *Proceedings of Empirical Methods for Natural Language Processing (EMNLP)*.

Sali A. Tagliamonte and Alexandra D'Arcy. 2009. Peaks beyond phonology: Adolescence, incrementation, and language change. *Language*, 85(1):58–108.

Nina Tahmasebi, Lars Borin, and Adam Jatowt. 2018. Survey of computational approaches to diachronic conceptual change. *arXiv preprint arXiv:1811.06278*.

Oren Tsur, Dan Calacci, and David Lazer. 2015. A frame of mind: Using statistical models for detection of framing and agenda setting campaigns. In *Proceedings of the Association for Computational Linguistics (ACL)*, pages 1629–1638.

Ted Underwood, David Bamman, and Sabrina Lee. 2018. The transformation of gender in english-language fiction. *Cultural Analytics*.

Uriel Weinreich, William Labov, and Marvin Herzog. 1968. Empirical foundations for a theory of language change. *Directions for historical linguistics*, pages 97–188.

Derry Tanti Wijaya and Reyyan Yeniterzi. 2011. Understanding semantic change of words over centuries. In *Proceedings of the 2011 international workshop on DETecting and Exploiting Cultural diversiTy on the social web*, pages 35–40. ACM.

Yi Yang and Jacob Eisenstein. 2016. Part-of-speech tagging for historical English. In *Proceedings of the North American Chapter of the Association for Computational Linguistics (NAACL)*.

Transfer Learning in Natural Language Processing Tutorial

Sebastian Ruder[1], Matthew Peters[2], Swabha Swayamdipta[3], Thomas Wolf[4]
[1] Insight Centre, NUI Galway & Aylien Ltd., Dublin
[2] Allen Institute for Artifical Intelligence
[3] Language Technologies Institute, CMU
[4] Huggingface Inc.
sebastian@ruder.io matthewp@allenai.org
swabha@cs.cmu.edu thomwolf@gmail.com

1 Introduction

The classic supervised machine learning paradigm is based on learning *in isolation*, a single predictive model for a task using a single dataset. This approach requires a large number of training examples and performs best for well-defined and narrow tasks. Transfer learning refers to a set of methods that extend this approach by leveraging data from additional domains or tasks to train a model with better generalization properties.

Over the last two years, the field of Natural Language Processing (NLP) has witnessed the emergence of several transfer learning methods and architectures which significantly improved upon the state-of-the-art on a wide range of NLP tasks (Peters et al., 2018a; Howard and Ruder, 2018; Radford et al., 2018; Devlin et al., 2018).

These improvements together with the wide availability and ease of integration of these methods are reminiscent of the factors that led to the success of pretrained word embeddings (Mikolov et al., 2013) and ImageNet pretraining in computer vision, and indicate that these methods will likely become a common tool in the NLP landscape as well as an important research direction.

We will present an overview of modern transfer learning methods in NLP, how models are pretrained, what information the representations they learn capture, and review examples and case studies on how these models can be integrated and adapted in downstream NLP tasks.

2 Description

The tutorial will start with a broad overview of transfer learning methods following Pan and Yang (2010). As part of this overview, we will also highlight connections to other related and promising directions of research such as meta-learning (Gu et al., 2018), multilingual transfer learning, and continual learning (Lopez-Paz and Ranzato, 2017).

We will then focus on the current most promising area, *sequential transfer learning* where tasks are learned in sequence. Sequential transfer learning consists of two stages: a *pretraining* phase in which general representations are learned on a *source* task or domain followed by an *adaptation* phase during which the learned knowledge is applied to a *target* task or domain.

Our discussion of the pretraining stage will review the main forms of pretraining methods commonly used today. We will try to provide attendants with an overview of what type of information these pretraining schemes are capturing and how pretraining schemes are devised.

In particular, we will review *unsupervised approaches* which aim to model the dataset itself, briefly presenting non-neural approaches (Deerwester et al., 1990; Brown et al., 1993; Blei et al., 2003) before detailing deep neural network approaches like auto-encoding/skip-thoughts models (Dai and Le, 2015; Kiros et al., 2015; Hill et al., 2016; Logeswaran and Lee, 2018) and the current trend of language model-based approaches (Dai and Le, 2015; Peters et al., 2018a; Howard and Ruder, 2018; Radford et al., 2018; Devlin et al., 2018). We will then describe *supervised approaches* which make use of large annotated datasets (Zoph et al., 2016; Yang et al., 2017; Wieting et al., 2016; Conneau et al., 2017; McCann et al., 2017) before turning to *distant supervision approaches* which use heuristics to automatically label datasets (Mintz et al., 2009; Severyn and Moschitti, 2015; Felbo et al., 2017; Yang et al., 2017).

Our review of distant supervision approaches will aim to provide attendants with a sense of how they can design heuristics that can automatically provide supervision in their own applications. Last

Proceedings of NAACL HLT 2019: Tutorial Abstracts, pages 15–18
Minneapolis, Minnesota, June 2, 2019.

but not least, we will highlight the use of multi-task learning for pretraining (Subramanian et al., 2018; Cer et al., 2018; Devlin et al., 2018).

This review of pretraining approaches will provide recommendations and discuss trade-offs of pretraining tasks based on our own experiments and recent studies (Zhang and Bowman, 2018; Anonymous, 2019).

We will then shed some light on what the learned representations can and cannot capture based on recent studies (Conneau et al., 2018; Peters et al., 2018b). We will discuss trade-offs between different modelling architectures and highlight the capabilities and deficiencies of individual models.

In the second part of the tutorial, we will focus on the second phase of sequential training, the *adaptation* phase as well as downstream applications. The adaptation phase involves a growing panel of methods:

Architecture modifications can range from a few additional embeddings to additional layers on top of the pre-trained to the insertion of intervening layers or modules inside the pre-trained model.

Optimization schedules for the adaptation phase can involve fine-tuning a varying portion of the pre-trained model (Long et al., 2015; Felbo et al., 2017; Howard and Ruder, 2018) with specifically designed regularization (Wiese et al., 2017; Kirkpatrick et al., 2017) or even fine-tuning in sequence a model on a series of datasets using several training objectives. We will summarize current trends in adapting pre-trained model to target tasks while highlighting best practices when they can be identified.

We will then focus on a selection of downstream applications such as classification (Howard and Ruder, 2018), natural language generation, structured prediction (Swayamdipta et al., 2018) or other classification tasks (Peters et al., 2018a; Devlin et al., 2018). This part will comprise hands-on examples designed around representative tasks and typical transfer learning schemes as detailed before. We will aim to demonstrate through practical examples how NLP researchers and practitioners can adapt these models to their own applications and provide them with a set of guidelines for practical usage.

Finally, we will present open problems, challenges, and directions in transfer learning for NLP.

3 Outline

This tutorial will be 3 hours long.

1. **Introduction** (15 minutes long): This section will introduce the theme of the tutorial: how transfer learning is used in current NLP. It will position sequential transfer learning among different transfer learning areas.

2. **Pretraining** (35 minutes): We will discuss unsupervised, supervised, and distantly supervised pretraining methods. As part of the unsupervised methods, we will also highlight seminal NLP approaches, such as LSA and Brown clusters.

3. **What do the representations capture** (20 minutes): Before discussing how the pretrained representations can be used in downstream tasks, we will discuss ways to analyze the representations and what properties they have been observed to capture.

4. **Break** (20 minutes)

5. **Adaptation** (30 minutes): In this section, we will present several ways to adapt these representations, feature extraction and fine-tuning. We will discuss practical considerations such as learning rate schedules, architecture modifications, etc.

6. **Down-stream applications** (40 minutes): In this section, we will highlight how pretrained representations have been used in different downstream tasks, such as text classification, natural language generation, structured prediction, among others. We will present hands-on examples and discuss best practices for each category of tasks.

7. **Open problems and directions** (20 minutes): In this final section, we will provide an outlook into the future. We will highlight both open problems and point to future research directions.

4 Prerequisites

- Machine Learning: Basic knowledge of common recent neural network architectures like RNN, CNN, and Transformers.

- Computational linguistics: Familiarity with standard NLP tasks such as text classification, natural language generation, and structured prediction.

5 Tutorial instructor information

Sebastian Ruder Sebastian Ruder is a research scientist at DeepMind. His research focuses on transfer learning in NLP. He has published widely read reviews of related areas, such as multi-task learning and cross-lingual word embeddings and co-organized the NLP Session at the Deep Learning Indaba 2018.

Matthew Peters Matthew Peters is a research scientist at AI2 focusing on large scale representation learning for NLP.

Swabha Swayamdipta Swabha Swayamdipta is a PhD student at the Language Technologies Institute at Carnegie Mellon University (currently a visiting student at University of Washington). Her primary research interests are developing efficient algorithms for structured prediction, with a focus on incorporating inductive biases from syntactic sources.

Thomas Wolf Thomas Wolf leads the Science Team at Huggingface, a Brooklyn-based startup working on open-domain dialog. He has open-sourced several widely used libraries for coreference resolution and transfer learning models in NLP and maintains a blog with practical tips for training large-scale transfer-learning and meta-learning models. His primary research interest is Natural Language Generation.

6 Audience size estimate

Due to the broad appeal and relevancy of the content of our tutorial, we expect a large audience, around 200 people.

References

Anonymous. 2019. Looking for ELMo's friends: Sentence-Level Pretraining Beyond Language Modeling.

David M. Blei, Andrew Y. Ng, and Michael I. Jordan. 2003. Latent Dirichlet Allocation. *Journal of Machine Learning Research*, 3(4-5):993–1022.

Peter F. Brown, Stephen Della Pietra, Vincent J. Della Pietra, and Robert L. Mercer. 1993. The mathematics of statistical machine translation: Parameter estimation. *Computational Linguistics*, 19(2):263–311.

Daniel Cer, Yinfei Yang, Sheng-yi Kong, Nan Hua, and Nicole Limtiaco. 2018. Universal Sentence Encoder.

Alexis Conneau, Douwe Kiela, Holger Schwenk, Loïc Barrault, and Antoine Bordes. 2017. Supervised Learning of Universal Sentence Representations from Natural Language Inference Data. In *Proceedings of the 2017 Conference on Empirical Methods in Natural Language Processing*.

Alexis Conneau, German Kruszewski, Guillaume Lample, Loïc Barrault, and Marco Baroni. 2018. What you can cram into a single vector: Probing sentence embeddings for linguistic properties. In *Proceedings of ACL 2018*.

Andrew M. Dai and Quoc V. Le. 2015. Semi-supervised Sequence Learning. *Advances in Neural Information Processing Systems (NIPS '15)*.

Scott Deerwester, Susan T Dumais, George W Furnas, Thomas K Landauer, and Richard Harshman. 1990. Indexing by latent semantic analysis. *Journal of the American society for information science*, 41(6):391–407.

Jacob Devlin, Ming-Wei Chang, Kenton Lee, and Kristina Toutanova. 2018. BERT: Pre-training of Deep Bidirectional Transformers for Language Understanding.

Bjarke Felbo, Alan Mislove, Anders Søgaard, Iyad Rahwan, and Sune Lehmann. 2017. Using millions of emoji occurrences to learn any-domain representations for detecting sentiment, emotion and sarcasm. In *Proceedings of the 2017 Conference on Empirical Methods in Natural Language Processing*.

Jiatao Gu, Yong Wang, Yun Chen, Kyunghyun Cho, and Victor O K Li. 2018. Meta-Learning for Low-Resource Neural Machine Translation. In *Proceedings of EMNLP 2018*.

Felix Hill, Kyunghyun Cho, and Anna Korhonen. 2016. Learning Distributed Representations of Sentences from Unlabelled Data. In *NAACL-HLT*.

Jeremy Howard and Sebastian Ruder. 2018. Universal Language Model Fine-tuning for Text Classification. In *Proceedings of ACL 2018*.

James Kirkpatrick, Razvan Pascanu, Neil Rabinowitz, Joel Veness, Guillaume Desjardins, Andrei A Rusu, Kieran Milan, John Quan, Tiago Ramalho, Agnieszka Grabska-Barwinska, Demis Hassabis, Claudia Clopath, Dharshan Kumaran, and Raia Hadsell. 2017. Overcoming catastrophic forgetting in neural networks. *PNAS*.

Ryan Kiros, Yukun Zhu, Ruslan Salakhutdinov, Richard S. Zemel, Antonio Torralba, Raquel Urtasun, and Sanja Fidler. 2015. Skip-Thought Vectors. In *Proceedings of NIPS 2015*.

Lajanugen Logeswaran and Honglak Lee. 2018. An efficient framework for learning sentence representations. In *Proceedings of ICLR 2018*.

Mingsheng Long, Yue Cao, Jianmin Wang, and Michael I. Jordan. 2015. Learning Transferable Features with Deep Adaptation Networks. In *Proceedings of ICML*, volume 37, Lille, France.

David Lopez-Paz and Marc'Aurelio Ranzato. 2017. Gradient Episodic Memory for Continuum Learning. In *Proceedings of NIPS 2017*.

Bryan McCann, James Bradbury, Caiming Xiong, and Richard Socher. 2017. Learned in Translation: Contextualized Word Vectors. In *Advances in Neural Information Processing Systems*.

Tomas Mikolov, Kai Chen, Greg Corrado, and Jeffrey Dean. 2013. Distributed Representations of Words and Phrases and their Compositionality. In *Advances in Neural Information Processing Systems*.

Mike Mintz, Steven Bills, Rion Snow, and Dan Jurafsky. 2009. Distant supervision for relation extraction without labeled data. In *Proceedings of the 47th Annual Meeting of the ACL and the 4th IJCNLP of the AFNLP*, pages 1003–1011.

Sinno Jialin Pan and Qiang Yang. 2010. A survey on transfer learning. *IEEE Transactions on Knowledge and Data Engineering*, 22(10):1345–1359.

Matthew E. Peters, Mark Neumann, Mohit Iyyer, Matt Gardner, Christopher Clark, Kenton Lee, and Luke Zettlemoyer. 2018a. Deep contextualized word representations. In *Proceedings of NAACL-HLT 2018*.

Matthew E Peters, Mark Neumann, Luke Zettlemoyer, Wen-tau Yih, Paul G Allen, and Computer Science. 2018b. Dissecting Contextual Word Embeddings: Architecture and Representation. In *Proceedings of EMNLP 2018*.

Alec Radford, Karthik Narasimhan, Tim Salimans, and Ilya Sutskever. 2018. Improving Language Understanding by Generative Pre-Training.

Aliaksei Severyn and Alessandro Moschitti. 2015. UNITN: Training Deep Convolutional Neural Network for Twitter Sentiment Classification. *Proceedings of the 9th International Workshop on Semantic Evaluation (SemEval 2015)*, pages 464–469.

Sandeep Subramanian, Adam Trischler, Yoshua Bengio, and Christopher J Pal. 2018. Learning General Purpose Distributed Sentence Representations via Large Scale Multi-task Learning. In *Proceedings of ICLR 2018*.

Swabha Swayamdipta, Sam Thomson, Kenton Lee, Luke Zettlemoyer, Chris Dyer, and Noah A. Smith. 2018. Syntactic Scaffolds for Semantic Structures. In *Proceedings of EMNLP 2018*.

Georg Wiese, Dirk Weissenborn, and Mariana Neves. 2017. Neural Domain Adaptation for Biomedical Question Answering. In *Proceedings of the 21st Conference on Computational Natural Language Learning (CoNLL 2017)*.

John Wieting, Mohit Bansal, Kevin Gimpel, and Karen Livescu. 2016. Towards Universal Paraphrastic Sentence Embeddings. In *Proceedings of ICLR*.

Jie Yang, Yue Zhang, and Fei Dong. 2017. Neural Word Segmentation with Rich Pretraining. In *Proceedings of the 55th Annual Meeting of the Association for Computational Linguistics (ACL 2017)*.

Kelly W Zhang and Samuel R Bowman. 2018. Language Modeling Teaches You More Syntax than Translation Does: Lessons Learned Through Auxiliary Task Analysis. *arXiv preprint arXiv:1809.10040*.

Barret Zoph, Deniz Yuret, Jonathan May, and Kevin Knight. 2016. Transfer Learning for Low-Resource Neural Machine Translation. In *Proceedings of EMNLP 2016*.

Language Learning and Processing in People and Machines

Aida Nematzadeh
DeepMind
nematzadeh@google.com

Richard Futrell
UC Irvine
rfutrell@uci.edu

Roger Levy
MIT
rplevy@mit.edu

1 A Brief Description

The ambitious goal of computational linguistics (CL) is to develop systems that process, understand, and produce natural languages. To achieve this goal, most work in CL has focused on developing models for different linguistic tasks such as semantic role labeling and natural language inference. However, recent research in CL has started investigating the missing ingredients required to move towards building systems with general linguistic intelligence. For example, one area of focus is multitask learning – building models that perform well on a number of linguistic tasks (*e.g.*, Devlin et al., 2018). Other research has investigated the importance of introducing commonsense into natural language processing models (*e.g.*, Rashkin et al., 2018). Despite the recent advances in the field, we are still far from systems that exhibit human-level linguistic intelligence: great performance on a set of predefined linguistics tasks does not result in systems that can understand and produce natural language in general settings.

An alternative research direction is to build systems that mimic language acquisition and processing as it is performed by humans. Such a system might achieve the linguistic efficacy required for understanding and producing human languages. But we first need to understand how children so effortlessly learn their language. A line of research aims to reverse-engineer child language acquisition: the idea is to shed light on the cognitive processes that might be responsible for language acquisition; we can in turn use the learned lessons in designing computational (cognitive) models that exhibit human-like language performance. Understanding language acquisition is also beneficial to natural language processing (NLP) applications: we can explore how the mechanisms (such as attention) and inductive biases that facilitate human learning can be explicitly incorporated into our algorithms. Moreover, we can evaluate our NLP systems with respect to human behavior which helps us understand the limitations of these systems.

The goal of this tutorial is to bring the fields of computational linguistics and computational cognitive science closer: we will introduce different stages of language acquisition and their parallel problems in NLP. As an example, one of the early challenges children face is mapping the meaning of word labels (such as "cat") to their referents (the furry animal in the living room). Word learning is similar to the word alignment problem in machine translation. We explain the current computational models of human language acquisition, their limitations, and how the insights from these models can be incorporated into NLP applications. Moreover, we discuss how we can take advantage of the cognitive science of language in computational linguistics: for example, by designing cognitively-motivated evaluation tasks or building language-learning inductive biases into our models.

We believe now is a great time for this tutorial. Using end-to-end and deep neural approaches has resulted in significant improvements in various NLP tasks in the past years. But in 2018, we observed a shift in the field from building models to creating datasets; this mainly happened because given the current compute power and access to vast amount of data, the existing NLP tasks were not challenging enough for our models. Revisiting challenges in language acquisition will spark interest in the community in two ways: Some will be inspired to design more challenging problems, and others may work on developing models of language acquisition.

Proceedings of NAACL HLT 2019: Tutorial Abstracts, pages 19–21
Minneapolis, Minnesota, June 2, 2019.

2 Type of the Tutorial

The tutorial is mostly introductory—we will explain the literature on computational models of language acquisition and processing. However, we will also introduce some of the recent research directions in this domain.

3 Outline of the Tutorial

- Introduction: the goal of the tutorial (5 minutes)
- Language acquisition (60 minutes)
  - Views/debates on language acquisition
  - The role of categorization, memory, and attention in language acquisition
  - Segmenting speech to words
  - Learning the meaning of words
  - Unraveling the structure of the words
  - Developing theory of mind
  - Understanding the pragmatics
- Language processing (60 minutes)
  - Methods and sources of data on human language processing
  - Expectation-based syntactic processing
  - Effects of working memory and computational models of them
  - Can RNNs explain patterns of human language processing?
  - Can incremental parsers explain patterns of human language processing?
- Cognitively-informed NLP (25 minutes)
  - Evaluating language models using psycholinguistic tests
  - Evaluating sequence-to-sequence models
  - Evaluating semantic representations and vector spaces
  - Evaluating question-answering models
- Language evolution (25 minutes)
  - Emergence of linguistic symbols
  - From symbols to linguistic structure
  - Recent agent-based modeling results
- Conclusion: main take-aways and future research (5 minutes)

4 The Breadth of the Tutorial

We will cover a broad range of topics in the computational cognitive science of language: the tutorial will mostly cover work by other researchers. The presenters will discuss their research when it is the most relevant work on the topic; this would cover less than 30% of the tutorial.

5 Prerequisites

To fully take advantage of the modeling part of the tutorial, the attendees need to have introductory-level knowledge of statistics, probability theory, and machine learning.

6 Instructors

- Aida Nematzadeh, DeepMind.
  - Email: `nematzadeh@google.com`
  - Website: `http://aidanematzadeh.me`
  - Research interests: I draw on the intersection of machine learning, cognitive science, and computational linguistics to investigate how humans learn language and use the insights to improve artificial intelligence systems. My recent work has focused on statistical approaches to semantic representations and theory-of-mind reasoning. During my PhD, I used computational modeling to study how children learn, represent, and search for semantic information.
- Richard Futrell, UC Irvine.
  - Email: `rfutrell@uci.edu`
  - Website: `http://socsci.uci.edu/~rfutrell`
  - Research interest: I study language processing in humans and machines. My hypothesis is that the distinctive properties of natural language, including its syntactic structure, can be explained in terms of efficient communication given human cognitive constraints. I explore this hypothesis in large-scale corpus studies, behavioral experiments, and cognitive modeling work using information theory and neural networks.
- Roger Levy, MIT.
  - Email: `rplevy@mit.edu`

– Website: http://www.mit.edu/~rplevy/
– Research interest: My research focuses on theoretical and applied questions in the processing and acquisition of natural language. Linguistic communication involves the resolution of uncertainty over a potentially unbounded set of possible signals and meanings. How can a fixed set of knowledge and resources be deployed to manage this uncertainty? And how is this knowledge acquired? To address these questions I combine computational modeling, psycholinguistic experimentation, and analysis of large naturalistic language datasets. This work furthers our understanding of the cognitive underpinning of language processing and acquisition, and helps us design models and algorithms that will allow machines to process human language.

7 The Audience Size

We expect an audience size of around 100. Roger gave a similar tutorial a few years ago which was attended by around 50 people. However, this was before the rapid growth of the ACL conferences.

8 Special Requirements

We require Internet access in the tutorial room.

9 Venue

We strongly prefer NAACL for logistical reasons; if NAACL is not possible then we would be open to EMNLP instead. ACL is not possible due to overlap with the Annual Conference of the Cognitive Science Society this year.

References

Jacob Devlin, Ming-Wei Chang, Kenton Lee, and Kristina Toutanova. 2018. Bert: Pre-training of deep bidirectional transformers for language understanding.

Hannah Rashkin, Maarten Sap, Emily Allaway, Noah A. Smith, and Yejin Choi. 2018. Event2mind: Commonsense inference on events, intents, and reactions.

Applications of Natural Language Processing in Clinical Research and Practice

Yanshan Wang
Mayo Clinic
Rochester, MN

Ahmad P. Tafti
Mayo Clinic
Rochester, MN

Sunghwan Sohn
Mayo Clinic
Rochester, MN

Rui Zhang
University of Minnesota
Minneapolis, MN

1 Tutorial Overview

Rapid growth in adoption of electronic health records (EHRs) has led to an unprecedented expansion in the availability of large longitudinal datasets. Large initiatives such as the Electronic Medical Records and Genomics (eMERGE) Network (Lemke et al., 2010), the Patient-Centered Outcomes Research Network (PCORNet) (Fleurence et al., 2014), and the Observational Health Data Science and Informatics (OHDSI) consortium (Hripcsak et al., 2015), have been established and have reported successful applications of secondary use of EHRs in clinical research and practice. In these applications, natural language processing (NLP) technologies have played a crucial role as much of detailed patient information in EHRs is embedded in narrative clinical documents. Meanwhile, a number of clinical NLP systems, such as MedLEE (Friedman et al., 1994), MetaMap/MetaMap Lite (Aronson and Lang, 2010), cTAKES (Savova et al., 2010), and MedTagger (Liu et al., 2013) have been developed and utilized to extract useful information from diverse types of clinical text, such as clinical notes, radiology reports, and pathology reports. Success stories in applying these tools have been reported widely (Wang et al., 2017).

Despite the demonstrated success of NLP in the clinical domain, methodologies and tools developed for the clinical NLP are still underknown and underutilized by students and experts in the general NLP domain, mainly due to the limited exposure to EHR data. Through this tutorial, we would like to introduce NLP methodologies and tools developed in the clinical domain, and showcase the real-world NLP applications in clinical research and practice at Mayo Clinic (the No. 1 national hospital ranked by the U.S. News & World Report and the No.1 hospital in the world by the Newsweek) and the University of Minnesota (the No. 41 best global universities ranked by the U.S. News & World Report). We will review NLP techniques in solving clinical problems and facilitating clinical research, the state-of-the art clinical NLP tools, and share collaboration experience with clinicians, as well as publicly available EHR data and medical resources, and finally conclude the tutorial with vast opportunities and challenges of clinical NLP. The tutorial will provide an overview of clinical backgrounds, and does not presume knowledge in medicine or health care. The goal of this tutorial is to encourage NLP researchers in the general domain (as opposed to the specialized clinical domain) to contribute to this burgeoning area.

In this tutorial, we will first present an overview of clinical NLP. We will then dive into two subareas of clinical NLP in clinical research, including big data infrastructure for large-scale clinical NLP and advances of NLP in clinical research, and two subareas in clinical practice, including clinical information extraction and patient cohort retrieval using EHRs. Around 70% of the tutorial will review clinical problems, cutting-edge methodologies, and public clinical NLP tools while another 30% introduce real-world clinical use cases at Mayo Clinic and the University of Minnesota. Finally, we will conclude the tutorial with challenges and opportunities in this rapidly developing domain.

2 Type of the tutorial

Introductory.

3 Outline

1. Introduction: Overview of Clinical NLP (10 minutes, Dr. Wang)

2. Big Data Infrastructure for Large-scale Clinical NLP (40 minutes, Dr. Tafti)

    - Motivation

Proceedings of NAACL HLT 2019: Tutorial Abstracts, pages 22–25
Minneapolis, Minnesota, June 2, 2019.

- Big data NLP: hope and hype
- Tools for big data NLP
- Case study: indexing Tweets data and health-related social media blog posts to trend analysis of cancer treatment strategies

3. Advances of NLP in Clinical Research (40 minutes, Dr. Zhang)
   - Motivation
   - Background of NLP to support clinical research
   - NLP Methodologies and tools for clinical research
   - Case study 1: family history information extraction
   - Case study 2: identifying use status of dietary supplements
4. Clinical Information Extraction: Methodologies and Tools (40 minutes, Dr. Sohn)
   - Motivation
   - Background of clinical information extraction
   - Methodology review: rule-based or machine learning/deep learning?
   - Tools and frameworks: UIMA framework, cTAKES, and MedTagger
   - Case study: ascertainment of asthma status using free-text EHRs
5. Patient Cohort Retrieval using EHRs (40 minutes, Dr. Wang)
   - Motivation
   - Background of patient cohort retrieval
   - Methodology: extraction of medical concepts, information retrieval for cohort identification
   - Case study 1: Patient cohort retrieval for epidemiology study
   - Case study 2: Patient cohort retrieval for clinical trials accrual
6. Clinical NLP: Challenges and Opportunities (10 minutes, Dr. Wang)
   - Challenges in methodology and practical applications
   - Opportunities for NLP in clinical research and practice

4 Instructors

Yanshan Wang is a Research Associate at Mayo Clinic. His current work is centered on developing novel NLP and artificial intelligence (AI) methodologies for facilitating clinical research and solving real-world clinical problems. Since he joined Mayo Clinic in 2015, he has been leading several NIH-funded projects, which aims to leverage and develop novel NLP techniques to automatically retrieve cohorts from clinical data repository using free-text EHR data. Dr. Wang has extensive collaborative research experience with physicians, epidemiology researchers, statisticians, NLP researchers, and IT technicians. He collaborated with rheumatologists and developed a NLP system for automatic identification of skeletal site-specific fractures from radiology reports for osteoporosis patients. He has had ongoing collaboration with epidemiologists and clinical neurologists on developing novel AI solutions to provide better care for elders. Dr. Wang has published over 40 peer-reviewed articles at referred computational linguistic conferences (e.g., NAACL), and medical informatics journals and conference (e.g., JBI, JAMIA, JMIR and AMIA). He has served on program committees for EMNLP, NAACL, IEEE-ICHI, IEEE-BIBM, etc. (wang.yanshan@mayo.edu)

Ahmad P. Tafti is a Research Associate at Mayo Clinic, with a deep passion for improving health informatics using diverse medical data sources combined with advanced computational methods. Dr. Tafti's major interests are AI, machine learning, and computational health informatics. He completed his PhD in Computer Science at University of Wisconsin-Milwaukee, and some part of his international studies were carried out at Oracle Education Center, Technical University of Vienna, and Medical University of Vienna, Austria. He won the General Electric Honorable Mention Award and received the 3rd place in the Larry Hause Student Poster Competition at an IEEE conference as part of his PhD project. Dr. Tafti has published over 20 first-author peer-reviewed publications in prestigious journals and conferences (e.g., CVPR, AMIA, ISVC, JMIR, PLOS, IEEE Big Data), addressing medical text and medical image analysis and understanding using advanced computational strategies. In addition, Dr. Tafti has served as a workshop organizer, steering committee member, technical reviewer, and a program committee member for several reputable conferences and journals, including KDD 2017, AMIA, IEEE ICHI, ISMCO, ISVC, IEEE Journal of Biomedical and Health Informatics, and International Journal of Computer Vision and Image Processing. He was awarded a NVIDIA GPU Grant for his accomplishments in deep learning community. (tafti.ahmad@mayo.edu)

Sunghwan Sohn is an Associate Professor of Biomedical Informatics at Mayo Clinic. He has expertise in mining large-scale EHRs to unlock unstructured and hidden information using natural language processing and machine learning, thus creating new capacities for clinical research and practice in order to achieve better patient solutions. He has been involved in the development of cTAKES, the most popular NLP tool in the clinical domain. Dr. Sohns research facilitates the best use of EHRs to solve clinical problems and improve public health. His work provides biomedical scientists and clinicians access to unstructured information from clinical narratives and clinical text analytics necessary for clinical research and patient care. Dr. Sohns research goal is the best utilization of informatics to facilitate translational research and precision medicine across heterogeneous EHR data and systems in a large population. (sohn.sunghwan@mayo.edu)

Rui Zhang is an Assistant Professor in the College of Pharmacy and the Institute for Health Informatics (IHI), and also graduate faculty in Data Science at the University of Minnesota (UMN). He is the Leader of NLP Services in Clinical and Transnational Science Institution (CTSI) at the UMN. Dr. Zhangs research focuses on health and biomedical informatics, especially biomedical NLP and text mining. His research interests include the secondly analysis of EHR data for patient care as well as pharmacovigilance knowledge discovery through mining biomedical literature. His researcher program is funded by federal agencies with over 3.5 million dollars including National Institutes of Health, the Agency for Health and Research Quality (AHRQ), and a medical device industry - Medtronic Inc. He also a co-investigator of a 42.6 million of CTSI grant. His work has been recognized on a national scale including Journal of Biomedical Informatics Editors Choice, nominated for Distinguished paper in AMIA Annual Symposium and Marco Ramoni Distinguished Paper Award for Translational Bioinformatics, as well as highlighted by The Wall Street Journal. (zhan1386@umn.edu)

Audience, Previous Tutorials and Venue

Based on the recent upsurge of interest in applications of NLP in the clinical domain, we target an audience of 60 to 100 students and researchers from both academia and industry. We are not aware of any recent tutorial on the topic of clinical NLP. No technical equipment is required. Since Mayo Clinic is located at Rochester, MN and the University of Minnesota is located at Minneapolis, MN, our preference for the venue is NAACL 2019 at Minneapolis, MN.

Acknowledgement

This tutorial has been made possible by partial support from the National Center for Advancing Translational Sciences (NCATS) Open Health Natural Language Processing (OHNLP) Consortium (U01TR002062).

References

Alan R Aronson and François-Michel Lang. 2010. An overview of metamap: historical perspective and recent advances. *Journal of the American Medical Informatics Association* 17(3):229–236.

Rachael L Fleurence, Lesley H Curtis, Robert M Califf, Richard Platt, Joe V Selby, and Jeffrey S Brown. 2014. Launching pcornet, a national patient-centered clinical research network. *Journal of the American Medical Informatics Association* 21(4):578–582.

Carol Friedman, Philip O Alderson, John HM Austin, James J Cimino, and Stephen B Johnson. 1994. A general natural-language text processor for clinical radiology. *Journal of the American Medical Informatics Association* 1(2):161–174.

George Hripcsak, Jon D Duke, Nigam H Shah, Christian G Reich, Vojtech Huser, Martijn J Schuemie, Marc A Suchard, Rae Woong Park, Ian Chi Kei Wong, Peter R Rijnbeek, et al. 2015. Observational health data sciences and informatics (ohdsi): opportunities for observational researchers. *Studies in health technology and informatics* 216:574.

Amy A Lemke, Joel T Wu, Carol Waudby, Jill Pulley, Carol P Somkin, and Susan Brown Trinidad. 2010. Community engagement in biobanking: Experiences from the emerge network. *Genomics, Society and Policy* 6(3):50.

Hongfang Liu, Suzette J Bielinski, Sunghwan Sohn, Sean Murphy, Kavishwar B Wagholikar, Siddhartha R Jonnalagadda, KE Ravikumar, Stephen T

Wu, Iftikhar J Kullo, and Christopher G Chute. 2013. An information extraction framework for cohort identification using electronic health records. *AMIA Summits on Translational Science Proceedings* 2013:149.

Guergana K Savova, James J Masanz, Philip V Ogren, Jiaping Zheng, Sunghwan Sohn, Karin C Kipper-Schuler, and Christopher G Chute. 2010. Mayo clinical text analysis and knowledge extraction system (ctakes): architecture, component evaluation and applications. *Journal of the American Medical Informatics Association* 17(5):507–513.

Yanshan Wang, Liwei Wang, Majid Rastegar-Mojarad, Sungrim Moon, Feichen Shen, Naveed Afzal, Sijia Liu, Yuqun Zeng, Saeed Mehrabi, Sunghwan Sohn, et al. 2017. Clinical information extraction applications: a literature review. *Journal of biomedical informatics* .

Author Index

Association for Computational Linguistics
209 N. Eighth Street
Stroudsburg, Pennsylvania 18360

ISBN 978-1-5108-8758-9

CURRAN ASSOCIATES INC.
proceedings.com